Snowbound

Snowbound

Dwelling in Winter

William Morgan

PRINCETON ARCHITECTURAL PRESS

NEW YORK

Contents

12
Mountain House
Manigod, France
Studio Razavi Architecture

20
Gaudin House
Les Grillesses, Switzerland
Savioz Fabrizzi Architectes

64
Einfamilienhaus Hochleitner
Embach, Austria
LP architektur

78
Rabothytta
Okstindan, Norway
Jarmund/Vigsnæs Arkitekter

120
One Year Project
Fukushima,Japan
ADX

132
Alpine Cabin
Vancouver Island, British Columbia
Scott & Scott Architects

174
Cabin on a Rock
Thornton, New Hampshire
I-Kanda Architects

184
High House
Saint-Ferréol-les-Neiges, Québec
DELORDINAIRE

30
Mountain Cabin
Laterns, Austria
Marte.Marte Architekten

42
Haus Fontanella
Fontanella, Austria
Bernardo Bader Architekten

50
Mylla Hytte
Mylla, Norway
Mork-Ulnes Architects

92
Atrium House
När, Gotland, Sweden
Tham & Videgård

100
Four-Cornered Villa
Virrat, Finland
Avanto Architects

110
DublDom
Kandalaksha, Russia
BIO-architects

142
Horizon Neighborhood
Eden, Utah
MacKay-Lyons Sweetapple Architects

156
Tre Søstre
Grand Marais, Minnesota
Salmela Architect

164
Cornwall Cabin
Cornwall, Connecticut
Resolution: 4 Architecture

192
La Leonera
Farellones, Chile
Del Rio Architectos Asociados (DRAA)

198
Rabbit Snare Gorge
Inverness, Nova Scotia
Omar Gandhi Architect & Design Base 8

208
Culardoch Shieling
Cairngorms, Scotland
Moxon Architects

Introduction

William Morgan

For the wolf-wind is wailing at the doorways,
And the snow drifts deep along the road,
And the ice gnomes are marching from their Norways,
And the great white cold walks abroad.

—Richard Hovey, "Hanover Winter Song," 1898

The score of projects in *Snowbound* illustrate that even the most beautiful cabin, whether perched on the side of a mountain, in an upland meadow, or on a screed of tundra, has, at its core, the theme of survival. Dwelling in winter requires an architecture that does more than celebrate the view: it must coexist with the elements.

From Arctic Russia and Atlantic Canada to the Andes of Chile, beauty depends upon design that is based on respect for a harsh climate. As pretty as snow can be, these retreats were fashioned to provide a sense of security, self-sufficiency, and control, so that the specter of perishing does not override the joy of habitation.

So many possibilities have led to the construction of these noteworthy houses and lodges in often remote and sometimes hostile places. Clients and their architects sought places to ski and trek, or just to get far from the madding crowd. Beyond recreation and vacation, some sought inexpensive land or less stringent building codes, or felt a desire to reconnect with familial roots. A few have even come to confront the very elements themselves.

All of these houses acknowledge nature, whether as a primitive force or as a metaphysical idea. The ancients called the northernmost part of the inhabitable world *Ultima Thule*—a kind of icy hell. Putting aside Scandinavia and the terra incognita discovered by the Vikings, it was not until the early Modern period that artists and writers embraced nature in all its wildness. Prior to the swirling, atmospheric snowstorms of the English romantic painter J. M. W. Turner, travelers traversing the Alps closed themselves within their carriages to keep out the terror of the mountains. The nineteenth century was an age of exploration, and polar lands were the last frontier. The dangers of the north were graphically epitomized in Caspar David Friedrich's 1824 painting *The Wreck of Hope*, which depicts a sunken vessel, crushed beneath sheets of ice in the Arctic.

Modernism and its Enlightenment foundations are interwoven into our relationship to nature, and how we find our place within it. Thomas Jefferson, Jean-Jacques Rousseau, and Edmund Burke, as well as the

Transcendentalists, all contributed to a shift from a belief in "man against nature" to more welcoming notions of recreation, with the Sublime serving up as much Byronic inspiration as fear. What history of modern architecture does not begin with Abbé Marc-Antoine Laugier's Primitive Hut? What contemporary environmentalist does not tip his hat to Thoreau's cabin at Walden Pond?

The projects collected for this volume are about design. If climate was the watchword, they are still the result of aesthetic decisions. Many of these retreats make respectful homages to indigenous barns, sheds, and other utilitarian structures. But they are striving to be much more. As elemental as the igloo of the Inuit, as practical as the log cabin—that ubiquitous frontier dwelling brought to America by the Finns—or as handsome as an alpine barn, these are works of architecture.

Yet, in their need to respond to the realities of high altitudes and latitudes, these structures stand on the shoulders of bygone builders. In a time of bloated McMansions, mannerist skyscrapers, and environmental degradation, these snowy shelters have reexamined what is necessary to survive and thrive amidst adverse conditions. Even with tremendous advances in new technologies and materials, sustainable architecture still depends upon time-tested practices of husbandry and construction. Our forebears in the remotest climates developed techniques to keep out the weather as economically and intelligently as possible. Houses and barns that did not take into consideration factors of siting, climate, and weather simply did not endure.

Not unlike the thoroughly less-is-more design of the igloo, the Lapp reindeer herder's tent, or the original Cape Cod cottage, most of the designs featured here are reductive. In their search for the essence of the winter dwelling, these designers have provided an antidote to the excess of so much shelter-magazine style. As the Belgian restoration architect Axel Vervoordt wrote, "The soul is discernible by the omnipresent void and silence of the snow."

Today's family weekend retreat will be different from traditional agricultural structures, but there are many correspondences. For example, the method of building a barn into a slope, originally to facilitate cattle feeding, is now reflected in an Alpine dwelling that employs a prominent overhang and puts living rooms above and sleeping rooms below. Understanding passive solar and the insulating properties of certain woods, reading the topography, and making do with limited resources: these were second nature to people living on the land before industrialization. How many of these new structures are attempts to recapture a predecessor's back-to-the-land spirit?

Beyond the certain verities—orientation, traditional materials, steep roofs, and building solidly in the face of heavy winter—there are major differences between the houses in this book and their forebears. Arguably the biggest difference is that these dwellings are not located where they are for reasons of heritage, though some carry an emotional, intergenerational link to their locales.

Tradition informs many of the houses. Culardoch Shieling in the Scottish Highlands has a grass roof and a form that harks back to shepherds' crofts. Rabbit Snare Gorge makes a nod to local construction techniques on Nova Scotia's Cape Breton Island. Einfamilienhaus Hochleitner and Haus Fontanella in Austria maintain local barn shapes, while Gaudin House in Switzerland was formerly a barn. Not far from Mont Blanc, Mountain House echoes the chalet style. The homes in Japan and New Hampshire employ age-old mortise-and-tenon wood frames.

Yet these traditional forms can be deceiving, for most of these houses rely upon recently developed technology. New materials and evolved systems make the houses tougher in their ability to withstand the elements, as well as possibly more affordable.

Horizon in Utah's Rocky Mountains has thermal mass concrete floors, while Bensonwood panels—with densely packed cellulose fiber for superior insulation—are employed in I-Kanda's Cabin on a Rock in Thornton, New Hampshire. Meanwhile, Cornwall Cabin in northwestern Connecticut employs the architects' revolutionary modular construction.

The real challenge of building in extreme winter conditions is illustrated here by two uber-remote trekking hostels, one in Norway and one in Russia, reachable only by foot or on skis. Yet climate change is diminishing glaciers and snow packs, and places such as the mountains of New England, Patagonia, and Australia have noticeably less precipitation on average each year. Candidates for *Snowbound* in Canada, Australia, and Vermont had to be eliminated as recent winters came with less-than-usual snowfall. In the middle of winter in the Southern hemisphere, there was insufficient snow in the Andes, more than a thousand miles south of Buenos Aires, to photograph a house as it would have looked only less than a decade ago.

What most unifies these twenty projects is their aspirational design. All were designed by architects as art. Some were built for their creators—perhaps the most revealing expression of an architect's design philosophy.

Some of the architects are well recognized for their work, particularly their responses to climate and culture. Designers such as Brian MacKay-Lyons and Talbot Sweetapple, along with Bolle Tham and Martin Videgård, and also David Salmela, have made noteworthy careers dealing with less than optimal conditions in cold and snowy places. The collection taps into a long tradition of climate-sensitive architecture in Scandinavia and Canada, with a series of felicitous cabins along the spine of the European Alps, from France to Austria.

Even so, these snow-wrapped ski lodges, trekker cabins, and mountain getaways were selected for inclusion not because of their designers' reputations or their locations. What unites these designers is their sensitivity to weather, landscape, and history. At its most basic, architecture is shelter, and here we experience its most refined form. The ability to withstand winter's harshness has been embraced by designers working both with age-old and revolutionary new materials to increase insulation and decrease reliance upon fossil fuels.

These twenty examples of winter dwellings and retreats represent a noble effort to marry architectural design with strategies for sustainability; they also share a certain modesty. There are plenty of over-the-top ski lodges around the globe, particularly in the American West. These are antidotes to those. The simple template of snow not only provided the challenge, but also the inspiration.

Mountain House

LOCATION
Manigod, France

ARCHITECT
Studio Razavi Architecture

COORDINATES
45.8612°N
6.3691°E

AVERAGE WINTER LOW
30°F (-1°C)

ENERGY SYSTEMS
Wood-burning stove; heat recovery ventilation; low-temperature heated floors

BUILDING MATERIALS
concrete, spruce (structure); pine planks (facade and interiors); lacquered steel (roof)

SQUARE FOOTAGE
2,368 SQ FT (220 M²)

COMPLETION
2016

Mountain House perches high in the French Alps, not far from Mont Blanc, and it evokes the traditional chalets of the Haute-Savoie region. Meaning to preserve the *patrimoine*, regional planning officials impose strict controls on new construction, dictating materials, windows sizes, and the slope of the roof. The clients, gallery owners and avid skiers from Paris, chose Studio Razavi because it was the only firm they interviewed that did not propose an old-style chalet. Instead, the designers achieved a reinterpretation of the good aspects of the past but in a thoroughly contemporary manner.

The spirit and order of the typical French alpine farmhouse, with animals in the ground level, granary above, and an upper story for family life, was replicated here. The top floor is reserved for living space, with bedrooms one floor below, and technical space, car parking, and ski gear stowage on the ground level. Progressively larger overhangs protect the vacation house from snow accumulation. As each floor gets more spacious, the fenestration gets larger (the windows on the uppermost level are set back to offer shade from summer sun).

Architect Alireza Razavi emphasizes both the traditional form and modernity. The upper floors are wrapped in pine, but there are surface variations to express the house's purpose and volume. The concrete base, however, is a real departure: local ordinances require stone bases, but the approved *béton brut* foundation reveals form board impressions, which contribute to a sense of alpine ruggedness.

Mountain House shares its sloping hillside with neighbors that mimic the older chalets, some with kitschy adornments. "Many of the houses in this valley," Razavi notes, "feature decorative elements applied for no real reason." One is reminded of the chalets designed by the young Le Corbusier in nearby La Chaux-de-Fonds, Switzerland. Mountain House is cleaner than any of its sources, and devoid of gimmicks. "We tried to express only the features that are essential to the building, and that keeps the overall aesthetic quite simple."

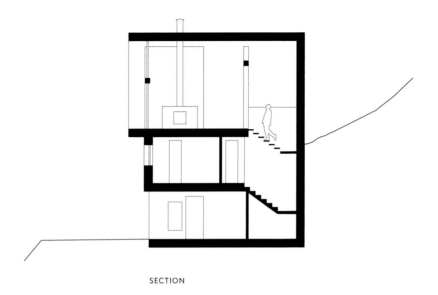

SECTION

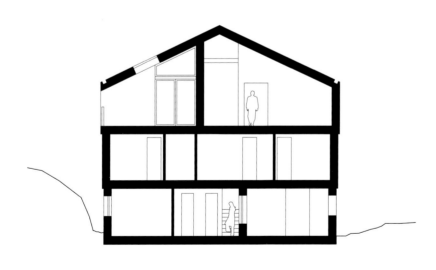

SECTION

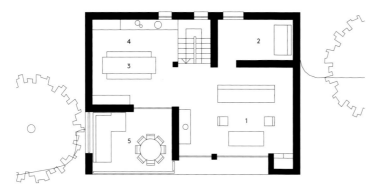

THIRD FLOOR PLAN

SECOND FLOOR PLAN

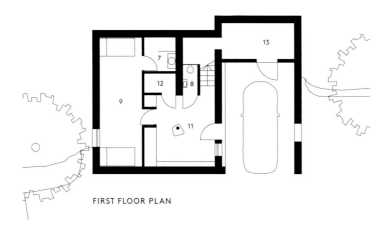

FIRST FLOOR PLAN

1   Living room

2   TV room

3   Dining room

4   Kitchen

5   Terrace

6   Master bedroom

7   Bathroom

8   WC

9   Bedroom

10 Sauna

11 Entrance hall

12 Laundry room

13 Boiler Room

10 FT

Gaudin House

LOCATION
Les Grillesses, Switzerland

ARCHITECT
Savioz Fabrizzi Architectes

COORDINATES
46.3095°N
7.4123°E

AVERAGE WINTER LOW
28°F (-2°C)

ENERGY SYSTEMS
Grid power; woodburning stove

BUILDING MATERIALS
Fir (structure); local stones
(exterior); corrugated iron
(roof); larch (interior walls,
floors, doors, windows)

SQUARE FOOTAGE
646 SQ FT (60 M²)

COMPLETION
2014

A large banner of glass unfurled across the front of Gaudin House announces that this stone barn has been transformed into a modern weekend retreat. Yet nothing else about the nineteenth-century, utilitarian agricultural outbuilding distracts from what the architects call its original "rudimentary character." Various annexes added over the years were dismantled to honor the original shape, with the architects respecting a sensible local sustainability that was already in place.

The lower level of the barn, where cattle were sheltered in inclement weather, now provides sleeping and storage. But the floor above, where hay would have been stored, is now a single open space complete with kitchen, wood stove, and room for dining and living. Boards of larch cover all the interior surfaces, their smoothness standing in sharp contrast to the rough stone that buffers the building against harsh alpine winters.

Everything in the living area centers on the single opening that looks out on some of the most spectacular scenery in Europe. This single strip of glazing, placed just below the eave of the roof, is more like a tapestry than a picture window. The slope of the ceiling focuses the view down the precipitous valley and across to the mountains.

The brilliance of the strip window reflects the architects' contention that the program must begin with the site, particularly "its place in the history and culture of a region." As a child, client Lisiane Gaudin used to visit her grandparents on this farm during the summer. Nestled beneath the Wildhorn glacier, the hamlet of Les Grillesses comprises a dozen barns, some abandoned, and some converted into holiday chalets. The Valais region today is devoted to winter sports, the area crisscrossed by ski slopes and trails.

The contemporary world of downhill skiing, now a major draw in the region, is a far cry from alpine meadow farming. This cozy barn conversion's rock walls and strategic siting, burrowed, as it is, into the hillside, reminds us that what is now a playground was once a place of hard work and rural isolation.

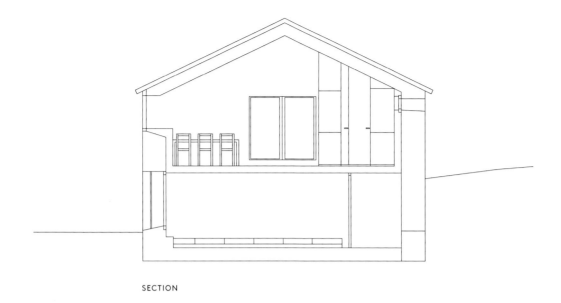

SECTION

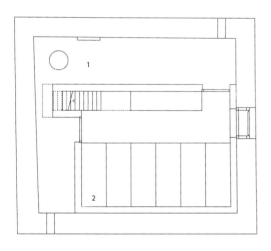

LOWER-LEVEL PLAN

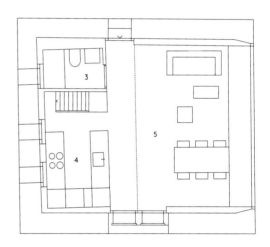

UPPER-LEVEL PLAN

10 FT

1 Technical room

2 Sleeping room

3 Bathroom

4 Kitchen

5 Living / Dining room

Mountain Cabin

LOCATION
Laterns, Austria

ARCHITECT
Marte.Marte Architekten

COORDINATES
47.2660°N
9.7051°E

AVERAGE WINTER LOW
28°F (-2°C)

ENERGY SYSTEMS
Geothermal heat pump;
woodburning stoves

BUILDING MATERIALS
Concrete; oak

SQUARE FOOTAGE
1,104 SQ FT (102.6 M²)

COMPLETION
2011

The Vorarlberg of far western Austria is tucked up in the mountains between Switzerland, Germany, and Liechtenstein. This alpine region, while known for skiing, is also an incubator of remarkable design talent. The clients for Mountain Cabin, a nature-loving dentist and his family, came to Vorarlberg natives Bernhard and Stefan Marte because they wanted something unlike either the traditional chalet or the contemporary ski retreat.

Their mountain cabin began with only one requirement: a sun terrace, but not one that would protrude out over the Upper Rhine Valley. This was achieved with a four-story cube, divided in the middle by two rectangular openings that form the sheltered terrace. This open area playfully mitigates the monolithic mass of the rough-hewn, pneumatically hammered concrete walls. So what might have been just another ski lodge reads as a geometrical puzzle, wherein the terrace becomes the starting point for a dynamic interior layout.

Reached by a drawbridge-like gangplank, the terrace serves as the home's *piano nobile*. Inside, a spiral staircase winds down to bedrooms and storage on the lower two levels, while another set of curving steps leads up to the top floor with its open-plan living room and kitchen. A single wood stove heats each zone. All the wood in the house is oak, including the square, deep-set windows that punch through the double-walled concrete shell. The fenestration frames the rugged outdoors like landscape paintings hung on the elegantly crafted, exposed concrete walls.

There is a geothermal heat pump, but the concrete sandwich construction with core insulation provides a tight envelope that can be warmed by just the two wood stoves. Along with the concrete, steel and solid oak construction ensure that the cabin is capable of withstanding an avalanche.

The overall minimal aesthetic is a contemporary echo of the simplicity of the local mountain vernacular, but rendered in pure sculptural form. Recalling a medieval tower guarding the steep slope in an opening in the dense forest, this mountain cabin is a fortress that appears defensible militarily—and totally sustainable. As the architects recounted in an interview, "we have not built a flimsy holiday house, but instead a place of retreat that will remain standing for generations, despite any forthcoming changes of climate and landscape."

Mountain Cabin   31

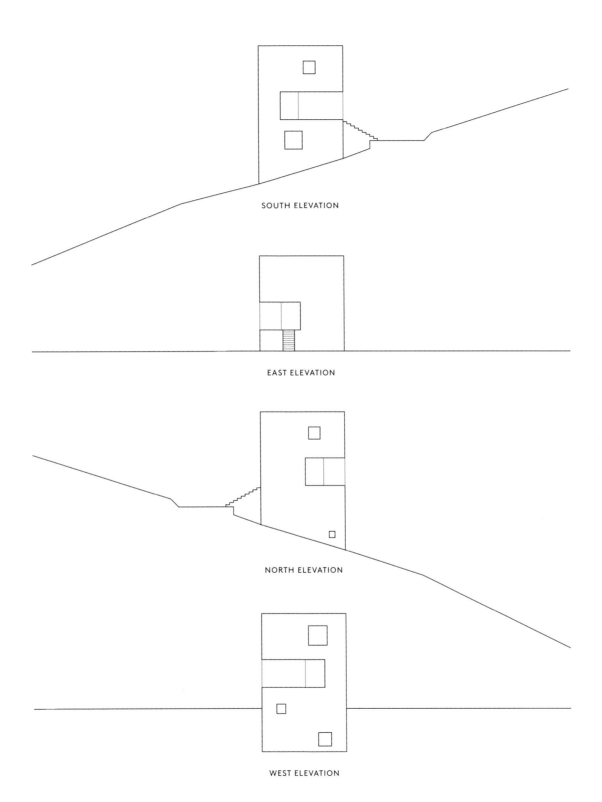

SOUTH ELEVATION

EAST ELEVATION

NORTH ELEVATION

WEST ELEVATION

Snowbound

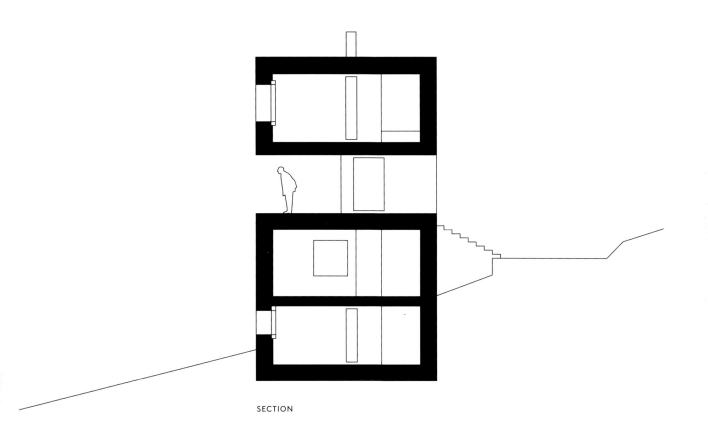

SECTION

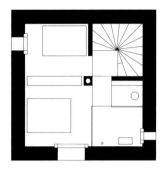

SECOND LEVEL

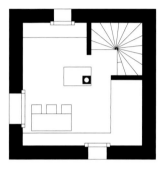

FOURTH LEVEL

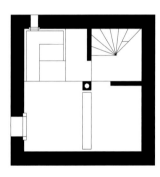

FIRST LEVEL (BASEMENT)

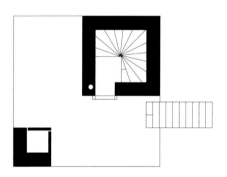

THIRD LEVEL (BALCONY)

10 FT

Haus Fontanella

LOCATION
Fontanella, Austria

ARCHITECT
Bernardo Bader Architekten

COORDINATES
47.2478 °N
9.9102 °E

AVERAGE WINTER LOW
28°F (-2°C)

ENERGY SYSTEMS
Geothermal heat pump

BUILDING MATERIALS
Concrete (base); spruce
(structure); larch (panels,
interior and exterior)

SQUARE FOOTAGE
1,905 SQ FT (177 M²)

COMPLETION
2013

The clients who commissioned Haus Fontanella were intent on finding an out-of-the-way village in which to settle. This international couple—he is from a city in Austria and she is from England—specifically sought a place where there was no airport. What they found is a hamlet with few weekenders. Their children can walk to the local school, which has only two teachers.

Fontanella is in the heart of the westernmost Austrian state of Vorarlberg, an area where the dialect is Walser German, a remnant of a tenth-century migration of peoples from the Rhône Valley. The Walser people, architect Bernardo Bader notes, "left behind a lot of valuable and sustainable architecture." Even so, this part of Europe, where Switzerland, Austria, and Germany meet, is fertile ground for exceptional contemporary architecture. The designer, whose office is in nearby Bregenz, was the recipient of the Piranesi Award in 2017 and a 2019 nominee for the European Union Prize for Contemporary Architecture—Mies van der Rohe Award.

This nineteen-hundred-square-foot family house in the country was a harbinger of Bader's large-scale and international work. While some of the neighbors regard the home as exotic, Bader's intention was modern *baukultur*, that is, today's version of the vernacular timber dwelling. "We talked a lot with the clients about traditional houses in the area," Bader recalls.

The three-story house intentionally has a compact volume, with the concrete base inserted into the hillside for insulation. Heating is provided by a wood stove and geothermal heat pump. Thus, Haus Fontanella is a triumph of energy-efficient design.

As sophisticated as these energy systems are, this village home still pays homage to historical regional tradition. The house is framed completely in spruce, while the exterior is sheathed in larch panels of varying widths, as delivered from the sawmill—"simple, first-hand, and rough," as Bader says.

In keeping with the aim of conserving as much energy as possible, fenestration is limited. Nevertheless, windows are strategically placed to frame distinct vistas of the surrounding mountains. Yet, one place where this cozy dwelling opens itself to the outside is the porch that leads from the basement sauna. From here, a bather may even interact with the snow.

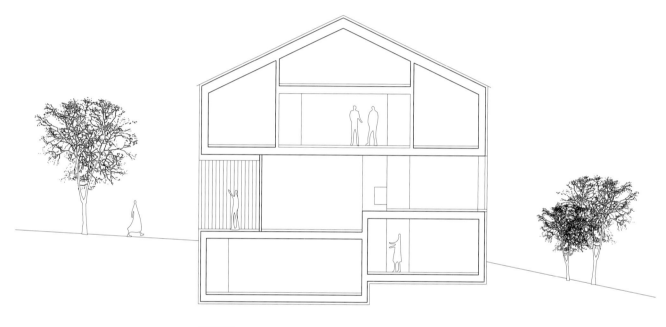

SECTION

LEVEL ONE

GROUND LEVEL

BASEMENT

1 Entrance/cloakroom

2 Kitchen/Dining room

3 Storeroom

4 Living room

5 Covered opened space

6 Stockroom

7 Room

8 Bedroom

9 Office

10 Sauna

10 FT

Mylla Hytte

LOCATION
Mylla, Norway

ARCHITECT
Mork-Ulnes Architects

COORDINATES
60.2415 °N
10.5509 °E

AVERAGE WINTER LOW
23°F (-5°C)

ENERGY SYSTEMS
Hydroelectric power; radiant
heat; woodburning stove

BUILDING MATERIALS
Heart pine (cladding and
roofing); pine plywood with
lye and white oil finish (interior
walls and ceilings, cabinets);
concrete (floors, bathroom,
countertops); solid pine
(windows and exterior doors)

SQUARE FOOTAGE
940 SQ FT (84 M²)

COMPLETION
2017

To have a second home in the country is ingrained in the Norwegian psyche. The *hytte* is often a small, barebones hut, a retreat for getting away from the city, a base for skiing, or a place for an urban dweller to reconnect with the forest. "Not being Norwegian," the clients, a family of four relocated from Houston, had no "preconceived notions or visions of what a hytte should look like." Nevertheless, the local planning code in the snow-filled Nordmarka wilderness requires a gable roof. But for this hytte the architect split the gable in half, creating four pitched roofs, in a pinwheel, or butterfly, configuration.

Program, site, and tradition, rather than modern technology, shaped this ingenious weekend house overlooking Mylla Lake. The basic elements of this 940-square-foot cabin are a compact footprint, precut framing lumber, natural wood siding, and radiant heat. "Our guiding principle," architect Casper Mork-Ulnes of the Oslo- and San Francisco–based firm notes, is "that the most sustainable square foot is the one that is not built." The demanding Nordic climate does not allow for shortcuts.

The multi-shed roof scheme offers two protected outdoor spaces while forming four distinct views of sky, lake, and woods from each arm of the pinwheel. The untreated pine planks on the exterior will register the seasons, and, in the architect's words, "turn silver over time— blending with the snow in winter and aging with grace in the forest landscape."

What appears at first to be a quartet of utilitarian agricultural outbuildings is an ingenious plan for a single residence that houses the family of four in two bedrooms and a bunkroom. Flush doors stored within the walls allow an open flow, but provide a relative degree of privacy when closed. Fourteen-foot ceilings, along with white-oil-finished plywood, make for a light and open interior. Elegant proportions are formed with the simplest of materials—walls, countertops, and bathrooms of concrete comprise the only other material. Team member Lexie Mork-Ulnes designed the furniture and the multi-purpose, built-in elements (the sofa, for example, is composed of two mattresses that easily convert to an extra sleeping accommodation). Such efficiency even allows space for a sauna and an annex for ski waxing.

The clients began with a list of specific request and amenities, but they fully trusted their architects, allowing the designers to "push the envelope of what a Norwegian hytte can be."

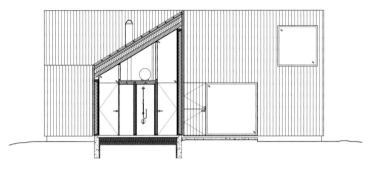

SECTION

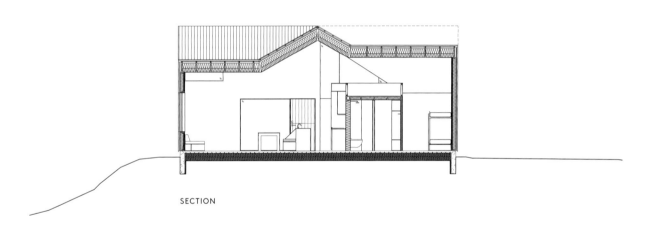

SECTION

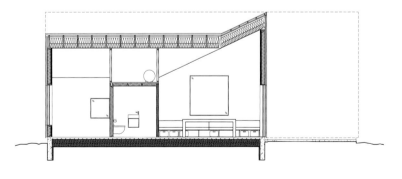

SECTION

Mylla Hytte

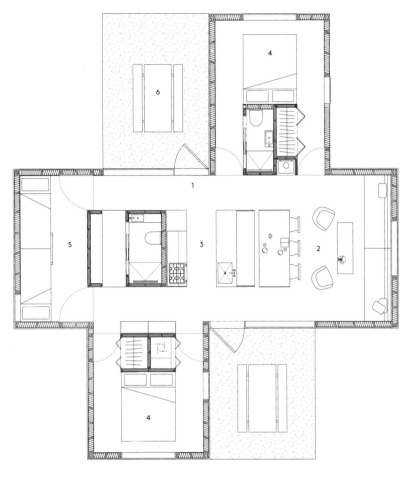

FLOOR PLAN

1   Entrance

2   Living/Dining room

3   Kitchen

4   Bedroom

5   Bunk room

6   Patio

10 FT

Einfamilienhaus Hochleitner

LOCATION
Embach, Austria

ARCHITECT
LP architektur

COORDINATES
47.2902 °N
13.0019 °W

AVERAGE WINTER LOW
22°F (-6°C)

ENERGY SYSTEMS
Solar power; woodburning stove

BUILDING MATERIALS
Concrete; wood

SQUARE FOOTAGE
1,130 SQ FT (105 M²)

COMPLETION
2016

Thomas Lechner, architect of this 1,130-square-foot house in the farming village of Embach, is a native of nearby Altenmarkt, where he has his design practice. While he was trained in Graz and has an international reputation, the mountainous Pongau region of Austria most informs Lechner's work. He teaches a course on wood construction at the University of Applied Sciences in Salzburg, and so it is no surprise that one of his wooden houses was the recipient of the Upper Austria Timber Construction Award for 2019.

The Hochleitners selected LP architektur for the firm's mastery of wood (Lechner converted a two-hundred-year-old barn, also in Embach, into a spiritual center). Like the other alpine examples in this book, the Embach house takes its cues from the region's rural vernacular: the barn's configuration, nestled into the slope, its snow-shedding gable roof, and its no-nonsense approach to successful building in a high mountain climate. Articles about the house, winner of the Austrian Architecture Award for Best House of 2018, carried titles such as "Minimalist timber cabin puts a modern twist on Austria's rural vernacular."

Except for the concrete base, wood is used throughout the cabin. The walls and roof are cross-laminated timber with high-performance wood fiber insulation. The rear of the house has a ventilated curtain wall of larch, a wood with a high content of natural oil that makes it especially resistant to weather.

The rough vertical sheathing presents a modest face to the world. But crossing over the metal bridge leading to an above-the-snow, second-story entrance, one enters a sophisticated contemporary interior, marked by soaring spaces and beautifully crafted wood walls, ceilings, and built-in furniture. The floors are oak, but all the other interior surfaces are light spruce. Planned around a central staircase, this organizing core—alluding to a tree trunk—allows a variety of floor and height variations; a large slanted skylight at the roof completes this unifying stem. Flanking the staircase is a two-story bookcase (Herr Hochleitner is an art historian and museum curator). The tower of books commands the full-height living room, and is illuminated by a giant window that surveys the village of Embach, just below, and the mountains beyond.

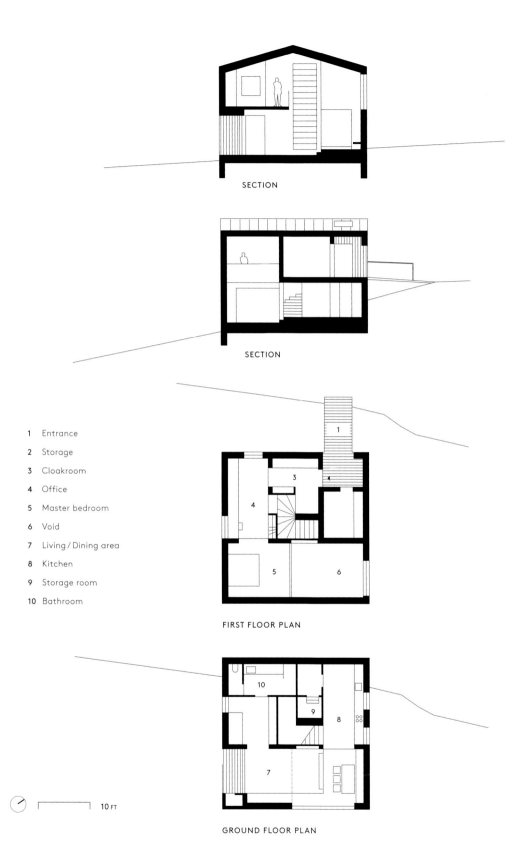

SECTION

SECTION

1   Entrance

2   Storage

3   Cloakroom

4   Office

5   Master bedroom

6   Void

7   Living / Dining area

8   Kitchen

9   Storage room

10   Bathroom

FIRST FLOOR PLAN

GROUND FLOOR PLAN

10 FT

Rabothytta

LOCATION
Okstindan, Norway

ARCHITECT
Jarmund/Vigsnæs Arkitekter

COORDINATES
65.9667°N
14.1667°E

AVERAGE WINTER LOW
18°F (-8°C)

ENERGY SYSTEMS
Solar power; woodburning stove

BUILDING MATERIALS
Concrete; glulam reinforced
timber beams; oriented strand
board; ferric-sulfate-treated
rough-cut timber; birch plywood

SQUARE FOOTAGE
2,153 SQ FT (200 M²)

COMPLETION
2014

Set among the highest mountains in Norway, Rabothytta is arguably the most isolated cabin in this book, reachable only on foot or on skis. And it is in a climate so harsh that a secondary rescue hut was constructed nearby in case the main shelter should be destroyed by heavy winds or a blizzard. Named for Charles Rabot, the nineteenth-century French glaciologist, ethnographer, and explorer who studied this mountainous region, the cabin can offer lodging for up to thirty trekkers.

In a place where it is too cold and too high for birds or insects, the behavior of the elements dictated the simple shape of the tourist cabin. Beyond the reach of the power grid, Rabothytta is powered by solar panels; two wood stoves provide heat. Entrances are prudently located on opposite sides; the insulating, gas pressure windows have been calibrated to avoid self-destruction at the four-thousand-foot altitude; and the plan allows shutting down half of the cabin to shepherd heat if dictated by dire conditions. Such dramatic measures give new meaning to building sustainably.

The boxed-in chimneys are the cabin's most distinctive feature, and while they echo the shape of the nearest mountain peaks, the enclosing pyramidal structures obviate the need for tension cables to secure the chimney stacks. The exterior is sheathed in thick timber boards, the finish left rough and treated with ferric sulphate to achieve its neutral gray hue.

That same rustic paneling was employed for the interior common areas. The birch plywood wall surfaces in the kitchen and bedrooms have been varnished in white. But the interior color scheme is mostly trekker-cabin-functional, with the intrepid visitors' anoraks and gear providing most plumage. The two living areas have double-height ceilings and walls of windows looking out on the glaciers to one side, and the lunar landscape of the mountain plateau on the other.

Rabothytta is one of the Norwegian Trekking Association's many unmanned cabins, made available for serious walkers and skiers. It takes an indomitable sort of adventurer who wants to match wits with nature at its most inhospitable, but such is the national spirit of exploration. The shelter offers succor from the elements, but it also provides front row seats for that mystical and cosmic display from the edge of the earth: the Northern Lights.

SECTION

1   Entry hall

2   Kitchen

3   Dining

4   Communal space

5   Food storage

6   Fire storage

7   Restroom

8   Bedroom

9   Children's play area

10 Storage

11 Technical soom

12 Mezzanine with bunk beds

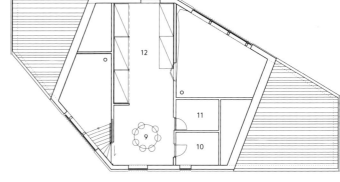

UPPER LEVEL PLAN

10 FT

LOWER LEVEL PLAN

Atrium House

LOCATION
När, Gotland, Sweden

ARCHITECT
Tham & Videgård

COORDINATES
57.2573°N
18.6351°E

AVERAGE WINTER LOW
26°F (-3°C)

ENERGY SYSTEMS
Wind grid power;
air-to-air heat exchanger;
hydronic in-floor heating

BUILDING MATERIALS
Lightweight concrete blocks
(structure); locally milled
concrete (foundation and
floors); carbon-blackened
plaster and oxidized zinc
(exterior); oak treated with
tar oil (windows and doors)

SQUARE FOOTAGE
2,287 SQ FT (212.5 M²)

COMPLETION
2010

Atrium House was inspired by the palpable presence of agricultural architecture in Gotland, the largest island on the Baltic Sea, where farming is still the mainstay. This strategically situated island has been a vital crossroads since ancient times, a stronghold from which Viking marauders sallied eastward, home to a major Hanseatic League port, and site of almost one hundred medieval churches.

Set in a sheep meadow at the edge of the sea, Atrium House was built for a couple from Stockholm with familial ties to the island. The living areas, designed to accommodate three generations of family, hug the outside walls of the square plan in a series of boxes comprising four bedrooms. Two of the sixty-five-foot-long sides meet in common areas of kitchen and living room. In turning Atrium House's back against the wind, the architects have created a building that supports its own microclimate: a sheltered but unroofed thirty-nine-square-foot inner courtyard.

A singular medieval fortress nearby provided local inspiration. Yet, the form is that of a Roman city house; an inward-facing atrium is as environmentally practical in a cold land as it is in a warm Mediterranean climate. Atrium House has a heat pump and radiant heating, but sustainability was primarily achieved through sound and efficient construction, drawing on passive methods used here for millennia.

Insulating concrete and masonry walls are stucco, blackened with carbon, while metal fittings are oxidized zinc. Tar oil on the oak doors and windows has turned them gray, to blend with the walls. The main entrance and portals to the atrium are hung with sliding barn doors, while sliding glass windows are mounted on the exterior walls. The limited number of these windows further emphasizes the sheltered, fortress-like mien of the home.

In winter, this seaside dwelling seems especially austere. Such minimalism reflects thoughtful adaptation to an old and otherworldly island; everything required for such a place is present, but distilled to a bare minimum. In its pure geometric configuration, Atrium House is classically modern, yet it acknowledges the genetic coding of Gotland's building history. Sophistication is only as good as its ability to sustain and enrich life in what is for most of the year a dark and harsh outpost.

Snowbound

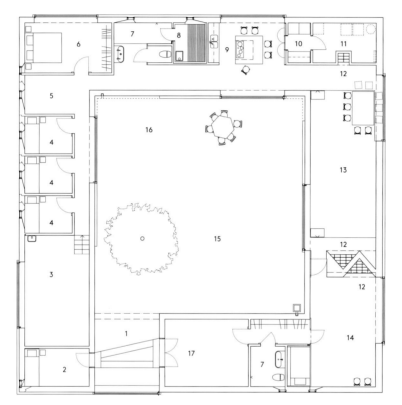

1 Entrance / Pergola

2 Guest study

3 Atelier / Workshop

4 Bedroom

5 Playroom

6 Master bedroom

7 Bath

8 Sauna

9 Kitchen

10 Larder

11 Laundry / Technical

12 Fireplace

13 Living / Dining room

14 Studio (Grandmother's room)

15 Courtyard

16 Terrace

17 Storage

FLOOR PLAN

10 FT

Snowbound

Four-Cornered Villa

LOCATION
Virrat, Finland

ARCHITECT
Avanto Architects

COORDINATES
62.2409°N
23.7702°E

AVERAGE WINTER LOW
17°F (-8°C)

ENERGY SYSTEMS
Solar power; twin fireplaces

BUILDING MATERIALS
Wood beams (balloon frame);
wood planks (interior and
exterior cladding); wood-fiber
insulation

SQUARE FOOTAGE
MAIN HOUSE:
840 SQ FT (78 M²)
SAUNA:
258 SQ FT (24 M²)

The retreat that architects Anu Puustinen and Ville Hara built for themselves on an island one hundred and eighty miles north of Helsinki speaks of Finland's second-home-in-the-forest culture. Even during the darkest months, the need to be at one with nature is one of the constants of Finnish life. Four-Cornered Villa also offers commentary on Modernism and pays homage to Finland's special relationship to winter.

The architects' firm name, Avanto, translates to "hole in the ice," and this is a place where one runs from the sauna to dive into the lake, even if that means using an axe to reach the water. To achieve a minimum impact on nature, this carbon-neutral home has no running water, and is heated by wood harvested on-site. Such sustainability, nevertheless, complements the cabin's artistic excellence.

Finnish architecture of the past century has primarily adhered to a rationalism based upon the straight line and the grid, despite a few detours by form givers such as Alvar Aalto and Reima Pietilä, not to mention the current worldwide trend for amorphously shaped buildings. Four-Cornered Villa's white-waxed interior of spruce and pine stands in dramatic contrast to its black exterior, which almost disappears into the trees. The flat roof provides, in Hara's words, "some warm irony to the clichés of modern architecture."

The plan of Four-Cornered Villa is a cross, with arms of equal length, offering distinctly different views of lake and forest. "You get morning light at the breakfast table," Puustinen notes, "midday in the dining room, and evening in the sitting room." The scrubbed whiteness befits a traditional country cottage, but it also emphasizes the geometric clarity of an aesthetic stoicism. Like many great works of art, this cabin is deceptively simple, yet mysteriously complex.

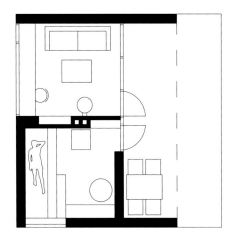

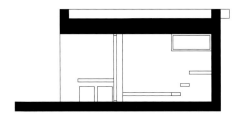

SAUNA PLAN AND SECTION

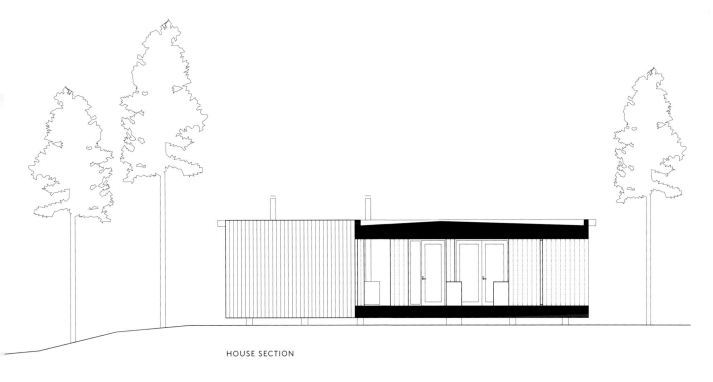

HOUSE SECTION

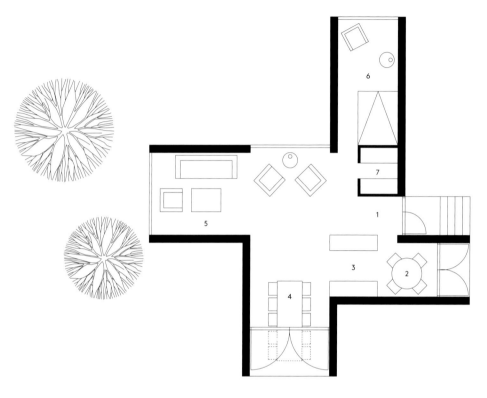

FLOOR PLAN

1   Entrance hall

2   Breakfast table

3   Kitchen

4   Dining room

5   Living room

6   Bedroom

7   Walk-in closet

10 FT

DublDom

LOCATION
Kandalaksha, Russia

ARCHITECT
BIO-architects

COORDINATES
67.1701°N
32.4230°E

AVERAGE WINTER LOW
6°F (-14°C)

ENERGY SYSTEMS
Woodburning stove

BUILDING MATERIALS
Laminated veneer lumber
(frame and some furniture);
polyurethane foam (insulation);
marine plywood (floors and
some furniture); plywood
finished with OSMO oil (walls
and ceilings); composite panels
and wood (exterior cladding)

SQUARE FOOTAGE
345 SQ FT (32 M²)

COMPLETION
2018

On April 13, 2018, a helicopter lifted this shelter for hikers, fisherman, and skiers across inhospitable tundra on Mount Volosyanaya in Russia's Murmansk region. A team then assembled the cabin in less than an hour. The circumstances demanded a structure that was both incredibly durable and extremely light. Given the Arctic terrain, it also had to be super energy efficient.

The two halves of this nature lovers' cabin emphasize the usefulness of a repeatable template for shelters in hard-to-reach places. Called DublDom, the modular, prefabricated shelter was developed by the Moscow-based BIO-architects, and made available in a variety of models. The ease of the cabin's construction, its lower building costs, and its compactness make it an ideal second home in the country. This particular DublDom, however, was a special challenge, as the cabin is accessible only via a rigorous trek in summer or by snowmobile in winter. Once reached, the rentable retreat serves as a refuge from blizzard whiteouts, numbingly low temperatures, and dangerously high winds.

Although solidly engineered to contend with the climate, the cabin sits lightly on the land, perched on a metal frame that touches the rocky terrain at only six points. The side walls are only two meters tall, but high enough so that the cabin can't be completely covered over by snow. Only the south wall, looking over the White Sea, is fully glazed.

DublDom is a single communal space, its 345 square feet large enough to sleep eight campers on simple metal bunks that line the walls. Accommodations are far from luxurious. Rather, the compact quarters emphasize the camaraderie of shared experiences in the wilderness. The hard surfaces and no-nonsense wall coverings stand in marked contrast to the paradigm of a contemporary sportsmen's getaway in the mountains. DublDom is at once transient and permanent, imaginative and barebones basic.

Centuries before political borders, generations of Sami reindeer herders followed their herds on migrations here. DublDom reflects the spirit of the Sami, whose own shelters are portable, low-tech, and adapted to survival in this brutal and unforgiving landscape.

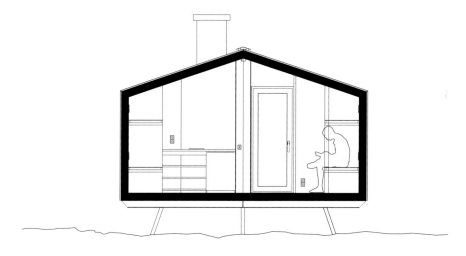

SECTION

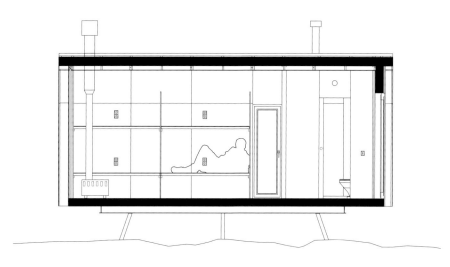

SECTION

Snowbound

FLOOR PLAN

10 FT

1   Main room with double beds

2   Kitchen

3   Bathroom

One Year Project

LOCATION
Inawashiro, Fukushima,
Japan

ARCHITECT
ADX

COORDINATES
37.5578 °N
32.4230 °E

AVERAGE WINTER LOW
26°F (-3°C)

ENERGY SYSTEMS
Air-to-air heat exchanger;
natural gas hot water heater

BUILDING MATERIALS
Bandai stone (foundation);
steel and local wood (structure)

SQUARE FOOTAGE
600 SQ FT (52 M²)

COMPLETION
2017

Architect Kotaro Anzai grew up at the foot of Mount Adatara, one of Japan's most historic peaks and a popular hiking destination. The mountain is visible from the office of his firm, ADX (formerly Life Style Koubou). This second home for city dwellers stands on stilts high enough to keep it above the region's six-foot snowfalls. Where possible, construction materials were sourced on-site, including the volcanic rocks upon which the dwelling's foundation sits. In an effort to honor the surrounding forest and provide shelter for future generations, new trees were planted to replace those harvested for construction.

In further homage to the spirit of the forest, no standardized, purchased lumber was used. After the hundred-year-old cedar trees were sawn, the wood was allowed to age. "Rather than just forcing nature into a method that is easier for the builder," the architect stated, "it is very important to build while thinking of the character of trees." As much of the log as possible was employed in construction, including the bark. Owing to the architect's methodical approach, it took twice as much time to construct One Year Project as it would have taken to erect a typical local dwelling.

Raised above the land, the house comprises two square sections with traditional Japanese hipped roofs and deep, protecting eaves. The smaller cube contains the more private world of kitchen, toilet, and bathing; small windows pierce wall panels. The larger block contains a bedroom and the living area, which is glazed on four sides. Connecting the pavilions is a pedestrian bridge, open to the elements. It is the designer's intention that this passageway compels "people to enjoy the harshness and happiness in the natural environment." The steel columns that raise the house above the landscape not only support the roofs, but also make possible the unencumbered floor-to-ceiling glazing and open living space. Set at various angles, these joyously dancing, tree-like columns are a metaphorical mirror image of the surrounding forest.

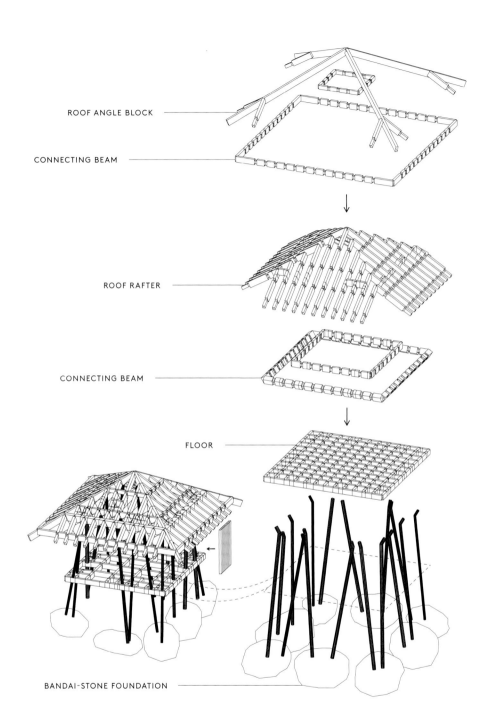

ROOF ANGLE BLOCK

CONNECTING BEAM

ROOF RAFTER

CONNECTING BEAM

FLOOR

BANDAI-STONE FOUNDATION

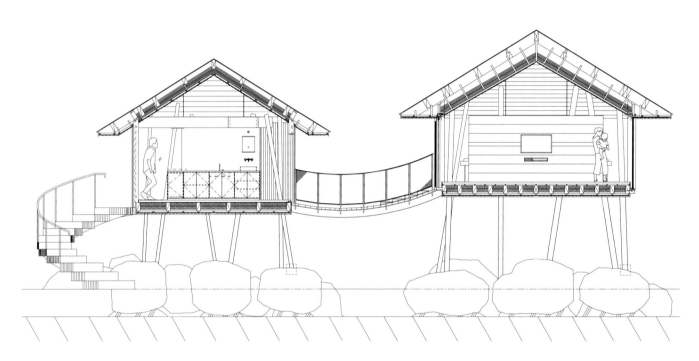

SECTION

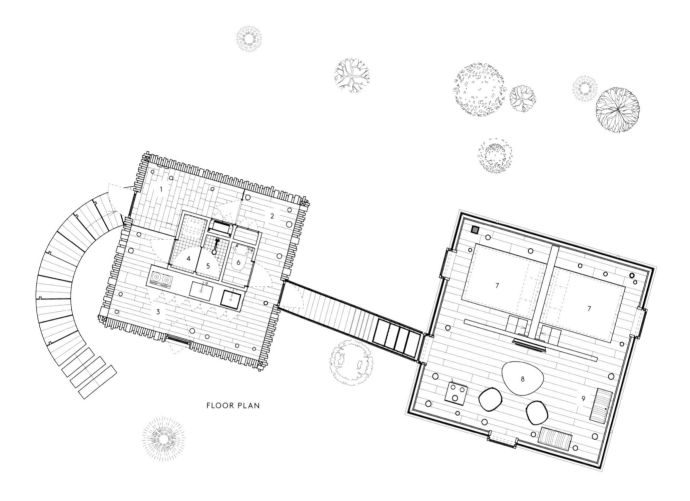

FLOOR PLAN

1 Entrance hall

2 Loft above

3 Kitchen

4 Changing room

5 Shower

6 Toilet

7 Bedroom

8 Living room

9 Firewood storage

10 FT

Alpine Cabin

LOCATION
Vancouver Island,
British Columbia

ARCHITECT
Scott & Scott Architects

COORDINATES
49.6506 °N
125.4494 °W

AVERAGE WINTER LOW
37°F (3°C)

ENERGY SYSTEMS
Woodburning stove

BUILDING MATERIALS
Local Douglas fir (structure
and interior); local Western
red cedar (exterior cladding)

SQUARE FOOTAGE
1,076 SQ FT (100 M²)

COMPLETION
2012

For an architect, there is nothing more elemental than building a cabin, especially one that will be reachable only by sled for half the year. If you plan to live off the grid, heat by wood stove, and haul water to a place where the annual snowfall reaches fifty feet or more, you must carefully consider every detail of your winter shelter.

Or else you must be young and daring, with the nature of a snowboarder, as were Susan and David Scott, of Scott & Scott Architects, who fashioned Alpine Cabin in the wilds of Vancouver Island, an hour from the nearest town, in the heart of snowboarding country. This, their first project, was formative, helping to define a practice known for "designing and crafting work in challenging sites where adventure is the reward."

Friends who share the Scotts's love of powder boarding and do-it-yourself spirit helped them construct their one-thousand-square-foot place in the Mount Cain Alpine Park Society, a collection of fifty-or-so cabins constructed over the past half century. Cedar cladding on the exterior has naturally weathered, while the fir walls inside were planed. The rough-sawn fir was harvested locally and excavation was done without heavy machinery.

The weathered boards, the simplicity of the forms, and the sloping roof, recall the shed-roof vernacular, most notable in Sea Ranch of the 1960s in northern California, or the design/build movement based at Prickly Mountain, Vermont in the 1970s. A likely influence came from the architecture of Nova Scotia, the designers having studied at Dalhousie University in Halifax. An inscribed copy of their mentor Brian MacKay-Lyons' *Plain Modern* was one of the Scotts' most cherished wedding presents.

Nevertheless, it was not aesthetics but structural considerations—resisting the area's strong winds and elevating the house above heavy snowfall—that determined the cabin's character. Environmental sensitivity was addressed by harvesting building materials locally to achieve the smallest possible carbon footprint. The Douglas fir columns, raw logs with the bark removed channel such iconic sources as Abbé Laugier's eighteenth-century Primitive Hut, not to mention countless homesteads across western Canada's mountainous landscape. But in the end, the alpine cabin is no more, and no less, than a handmade refuge for the winter sports maven.

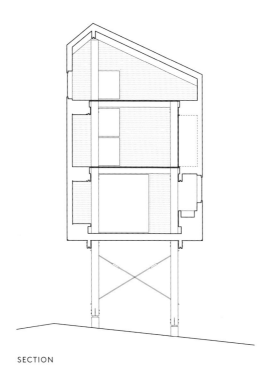

SECTION

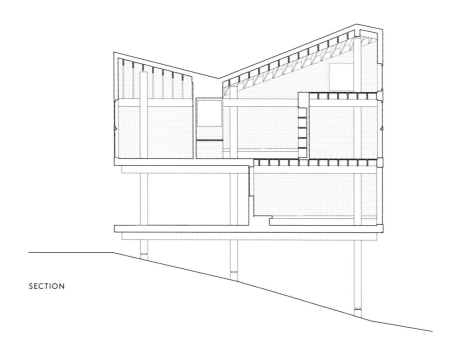

SECTION

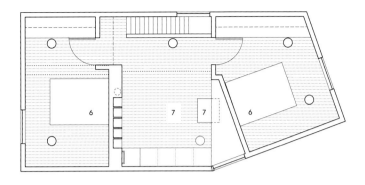

SECOND FLOOR PLAN

1 Living/Dining room

2 Kitchen

3 WC

4 Sauna

5 Covered entry

6 Bedroom

7 Den/Office

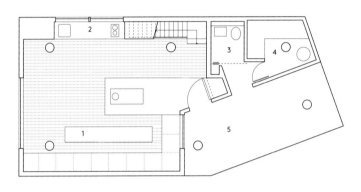

FIRST FLOOR PLAN

10 FT

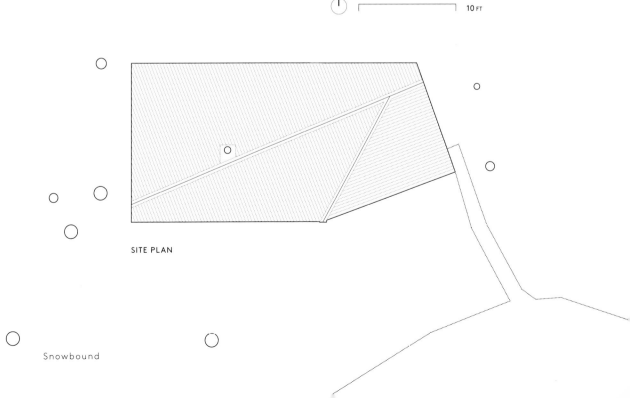

SITE PLAN

Horizon Neighborhood

LOCATION
Eden, Utah

ARCHITECT
MacKay-Lyons
Sweetapple Architects

COORDINATES
41.3007°N
111.7807°W

AVERAGE WINTER LOW
12°F (-11°C)

ENERGY SYSTEMS
Grid power; passive solar with
thermal mass concrete floors;
hydronic in-floor heating

BUILDING MATERIALS
Wood (stick frame); steel

SQUARE FOOTAGE
1,000–3,000 SQ FT
(93–279 M²)

COMPLETION
2019

A decade—and half the globe—separates the Horizon Neighborhood in the Rocky Mountains of the American West from the Canadian Embassy in Dhaka, Bangladesh. Yet, these two projects by MacKay-Lyons Sweetapple demonstrate this architectural firm's understanding of regional building practices, climate, and place. Springing not from New York, Los Angeles, or Dubai, but rather from back-of-beyond Nova Scotia, the architects have parlayed attention to the local into a body of work with universal resonance.

This collection of thirty cottages in Eden, Utah, the first project out of the Canadian firm's Denver office, offers a palate-cleansing alternative to the usual overblown American ski destination. More than just an elegant, dialed-back resort, Horizon is a planned community of social impact investors and innovators concerned with land stewardship and climate responsiveness. Designed around a series of courtyards, the layout intentionally encourages chance meetings and social interaction.

The cabins range from one thousand to three thousand square feet, and the protected communal outdoor spaces are formed by two orientations: parallel-grain (which follows land contours as would mountain goats); and cross-grain (which projects off the mountain like an extreme skier). Looking like a child's drawing of an alpine village in the snow, the development's shingled roofs and vertical cedar walls were inspired by the similarly sheathed barns in the valley below. Aluminum-clad windows meet at the corners, creating a crisp, taut building envelope.

This sense of lightness was further accentuated by elevating the cabins on steel stilts, a protective measure in the fragile, high-desert landscape where Horizon is situated. As Brian MacKay-Lyons notes, "In Canada we know about snow," but conditions at Horizon are "subject to many climate extremes: extreme annual snowfall, extreme wind loads, extreme solar gain," not to mention seismic activity. Passive solar orientation, hydronic in-floor heating, and thermal mass concrete floors contribute to climate responsiveness. Upper-level bridges on stilts ensure entry even in heavy snowfall, but these trussed elements keep the building's footprint light on the land, while minimizing the use of concrete. The structural frame fosters a sense of impermanence reminiscent of early Western mining camps.

As if nine thousand feet of site elevation were not high enough, the living areas are situated on the upper floors. Floor-to-ceiling windows embrace breathtaking views out over the Powder Mountain resort, the Great Salt Lake, the Western desert.

Snowbound

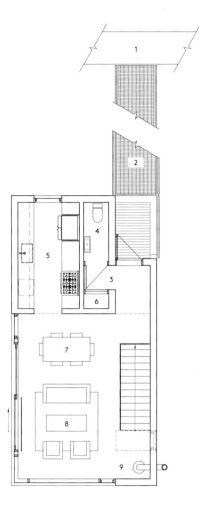

UPPER LEVEL PLAN

1 Shared pathway

2 Bridge

3 Mud room

4 Powder room

5 Kitchen

6 Closet

7 Dining room

8 Living room

9 Wood stove

10 Bedroom

11 Bathroom

12 Mechanical room

13 Stacked wood

14 Bench

10 FT

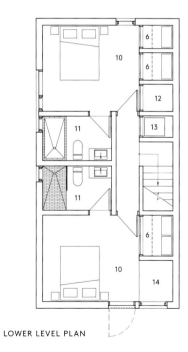

LOWER LEVEL PLAN

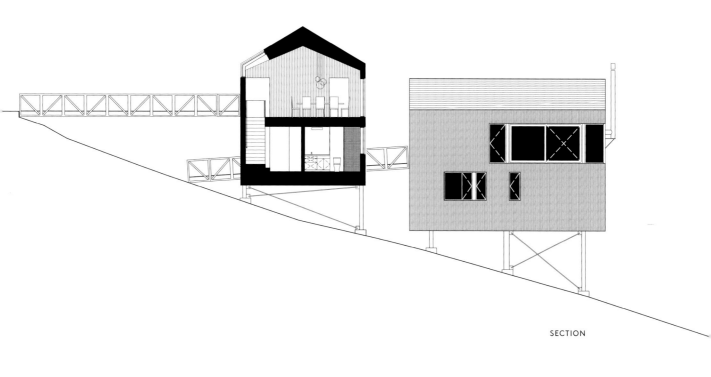

SECTION

Tre Søstre

LOCATION
Grand Marais,
Minnesota

ARCHITECT
Salmela Architect

COORDINATES
47.7531°N
90.3348°W

AVERAGE WINTER LOW
9°F (-13°C)

ENERGY SYSTEMS
Grid power; hydronic in-floor
heating; passive solar

BUILDING MATERIALS
Natural untreated cedar
(siding, exterior stairs, and
decks); painted cedar (siding
at base); black Vermont slate
(floors); Douglas fir (interior
stairs, slats, ceiling, and trim);
painted drywall; insulating
windows; EPDM (roof); Richlite
(entry roofs); dry laid stone
(landscape walls); concrete
(paths)

SQUARE FOOTAGE
473 SQ FT (44 M²)

COMPLETION
2019

Grand Marais, Minnesota, was founded by Scandinavian fishermen in
the early 1900s. Wedged in between Lake Superior and Superior National
Forest, this small town is sustained by recreational tourism—skiing and
hiking, sailing and sea kayaking. It is a remote, modest village composed
of low-rise commercial buildings, single-family homes, and short-term
rental properties. These rental units called *Tre Søstre* ("three sisters"
in Danish) reflect both the local ambience and practicalities of life in
an uncertain, boom-or-bust economy.

The clients, aware of Grand Marais' personality, wanted a
"contemporary architectural statement that prioritized views while
remaining sensitive to existing structures and the neighborhood
context." Duluth architect David Salmela, who has a notable body
of environmentally and culturally sensitive work, created a gaggle of
wooden houses that would not be out of place on a lake in Finland.
But the *gestalt* here is as much lumberjack as Nordic Modern.

Acknowledging the harsh wilderness country, Salmela has densely
clustered the trio amidst a series of dry-laid retaining walls that define
a "dynamic sequence of patios, softscapes, and circulation paths." The
goal was to preserve privacy and keep the buildings gathered tightly
together in the face of serious winter weather. The facades feature a
series of decks, with one over each entrance and decks at the second
and third stories (the ground floor is reserved for bedrooms). Since the
footprint is only sixteen by twenty-two feet, these outdoor rooms extend
the living spaces, while offering unobstructed eastward views of the lake,
harbor, and village. An additional south-facing deck offers a dramatic
perch, reminiscent of a crow's nest. These varied cantilevers add visual
interest to what are basically simple rectangles; their shape recalls
stubbor, traditional Scandinavian farm buildings used for storing grain.

In keeping with the modest rusticity, Tre Søstre is wrapped
in untreated cedar, chosen for its lack of maintenance. A layer of
structural insulated panels lies beneath the cedar cladding. Green roofs
adorn the garage and the storage building. The triple-pane, energy
efficient windows are a uniquely northern fenestration, designed in
Norway but manufactured in nearby Wisconsin.

The south-facing windows also provide passive heat, but their
sustainable and protective qualities fade in comparison to the
unparalleled views they offer of colossal Lake Superior.

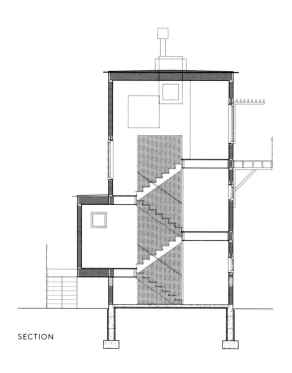

SECTION

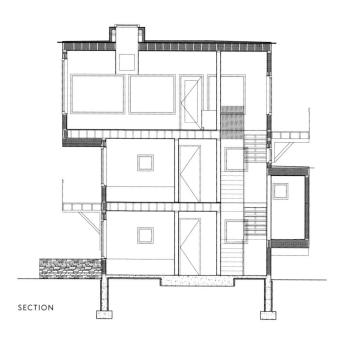

SECTION

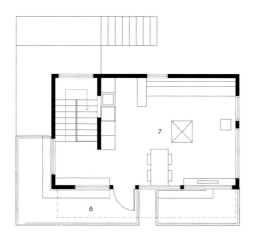

THIRD FLOOR PLAN (UNITS A&B)

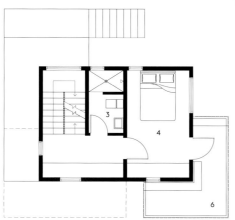

1 Entry porch

2 Entry

3 Bathroom

4 Bedroom

5 Patio

6 Balcony

7 Living space

8 Mechanical

SECOND FLOOR PLAN (UNITS A&B)

FIRST FLOOR PLAN (ALL UNITS)

10 FT

Cornwall Cabin

LOCATION
Cornwall, Connecticut

ARCHITECT
Resolution: 4 Architecture

COORDINATES
41.8437°N
73.3293°W

AVERAGE WINTER LOW
17°F (-8°C)

ENERGY SYSTEMS
Passive cooling (brise-soleil);
radiant in-floor heating;
wood-burning stove

BUILDING MATERIALS
Charred cypress (cladding);
cedar (ceilings); walnut
(millwork); porcelain tiles
(floors)

SQUARE FOOTAGE
1,500 SQ FT (139 M²)

COMPLETION
2017

Joseph Tanney and Robert Luntz, addressing another of their Modern Modular houses in Connecticut's Litchfield Hills, wrote, "Like the traditional homes that occupy the surrounding landscape, this modern home embodies tradition in the making." The same can be said of the cabin the architects built in Cornwall.

The early eighteenth-century town of Cornwall has fewer residents than it did two centuries ago. The area is rural, its upland elevation averages over fifty inches of snowfall a year, and its 1841 covered bridge is a New England icon. The area is far enough from the city to be *away*, but close enough to attract New Yorkers in search of places to erect second homes. Thus, amidst its scenic beauty and old homes, one finds contemporary houses designed by sophisticated architects.

As an example of off-site factory construction, Cornwall Cabin is more than just another handsome second home. Having set about to transform the "sub-urban fabric of the domestic American landscape" with their mass-customized houses, Resolution: 4 employs their conceptual building blocks to create efficient and sustainable prefab dwellings.

The designers' standard module is based on the maximum dimensions that can be transported on the highway. These manufactured LEGO-like blocks can be arranged in countless variations, connected, and finished on site. Despite the economy of means, no two of these houses look alike.

Cornwall Cabin is composed of two twelve by sixty-four-foot modules placed side by side; one unit is pulled apart, forming an enclosed porch in between the separated halves. This vacation house for a publisher is clad in cypress that has been burned and brushed following the ancient Japanese finishing technique *Yakisugi*, commonly called *shou sugi ban*. This charred wood siding is resistant to termites and moisture, extremely durable, and when coated in oil, can last a century or more.

Many Americans associate manufactured housing with trailer park tackiness and flimsy construction. Cornwall Cabin, however, offers a tight envelope featuring an array of sustainable features, including a green roof, high performance glass, and certified sustainable hardwoods. The client wanted more than economy and sustainability. She approached Resolution: 4 asking specifically for a house that would "embody a modern, low-slung cozy cabin, that is horizontal, rustic, finely detailed, captures exterior space with a covered roof, and has a brick fireplace as a focal point." The result is a modern house linked to a long tradition of satisfying winter-responsive design.

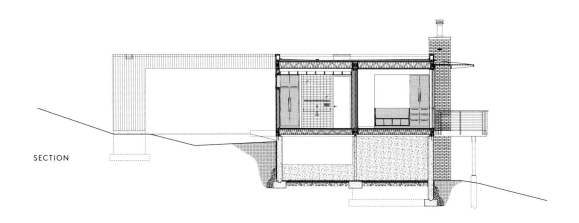

SECTION

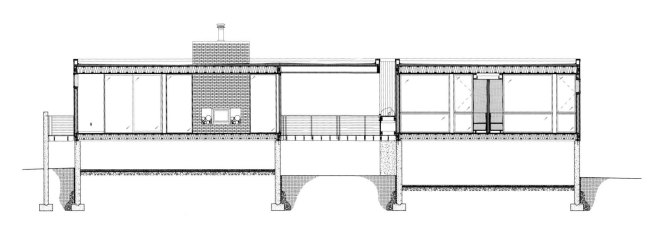

SECTION

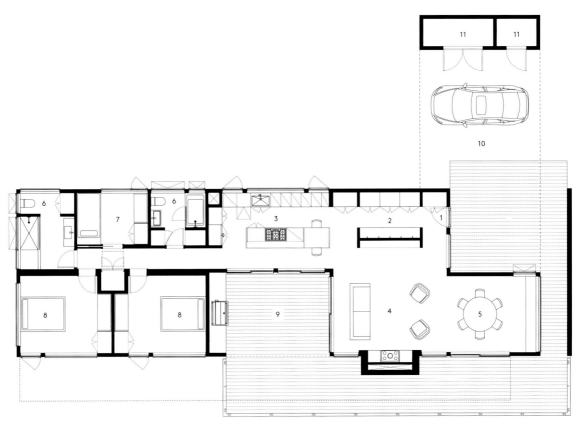

FLOOR PLAN

1 Entrance

2 Mud area

3 Kitchen

4 Living room

5 Dining room

6 Bathroom

7 Bunk room

8 Bedroom

9 Covered deck

10 Carport

11 Storage

Cabin
on a Rock

LOCATION
Thornton, New Hampshire

ARCHITECT
I-Kanda Architects

COORDINATES
43.8928 °N
71.6759 °W

AVERAGE WINTER LOW
8°F (-11°C)

ENERGY SYSTEMS
Hydronic radiant heat;
woodburning stove;
propane-powered tankless
hot water system

BUILDING MATERIALS
Wolmanized engineered wood
girders (structure); douglas
fir (interior timber posts and
beams); cedar (tongue-and-
groove wood siding); standing
seam aluminum panels (walls
and roof); mahogany (windows
and doors); Locally sourced pine
boards (floors and walls); slate
tile (floors, foyer, bathroom
and hearth)

SQUARE FOOTAGE
900 SQ FT (84 M²)

COMPLETION
2017

Presented with the unyielding topography of the White Mountains, the designers of Cabin on a Rock placed the building's foundation on hand-poured concrete footings; in doing so, they preserved the site's millenniums-old accumulation of igneous rock. This weekend getaway perches precariously on a steep slope, allowing dramatic views of several mountain peaks in New Hampshire's ski country.

Further limiting site disturbance, the architects employed prefabricated construction. All framing members were engineered and precut off-site. Along with the heavily insulated walls, floors, and roof, everything needed for construction arrived ready for assembly. This systematic approach meant the house could be built quickly, with minimal disturbance to the site and few trees sacrificed in service of a dramatic mountain vista.

Although small, the cabin is ingeniously configured to make the most of its nine hundred square feet. The rectangular floor plan was tweaked by skewing the common gable roof diagonally from corner to corner. This contributes needed headroom in the sleeping loft and also creates a faceted geometry. The overall plan resembles a morphed parallelogram, reinforced by wedge-shaped decks on the front and rear. The effect is of a cabin in constant transformation. There is no overt reference to the mountains, but the house's silhouette does reflect the firm's design process, and perhaps architect Isamu Kanda's structural engineering training, as well as his time working with Santiago Calatrava. "Geometric exploration," Kanda notes, "has always been at the core of our architectural practice."

The clients (one was a childhood friend and skiing buddy of Kanda's) planned a Thoreau-like cabin on land they had found in Thornton. During the design process the family doubled in size. Thus, the exterior decks were planned to expand the usable floor space considerably (at least in the warmer months).

South-facing glazing provides passive solar heating in the winter months, when the family, cozy, protected, and warmed by the woodstove, can contemplate the most mountainous landscape in the Northeast. Mountains to the east—Jennings Peak, Sandwich Mountain, and Black Mountain—form the cabin's breathtaking prospect.

SITE SECTION

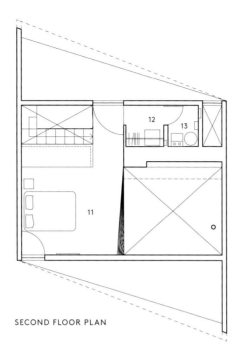

SECOND FLOOR PLAN

1   Entry

2   Living/Dining room

3   Fireplace

4   Kitchen

5   WC

6   Foyer

7   Bunks

8   Shed

9   Deck

10 Firepit

11 Loft bedroom

12 Laundry

13 Mechanical room

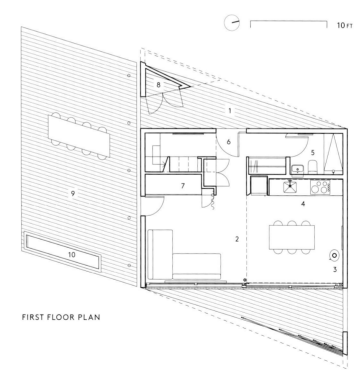

10 FT

FIRST FLOOR PLAN

High House

LOCATION
Saint-Ferréol-les-Neiges,
Québec

ARCHITECT
Delordinaire

COORDINATES
47.1169°N
70.8598°W

AVERAGE WINTER LOW
7°F (-14°C)

ENERGY SYSTEMS
Hydroelectric grid power;
woodburning stove

BUILDING MATERIALS
Steel (roof, foundation);
wood (foundation); concrete
(exterior walls, foundation)

SQUARE FOOTAGE
950 SQ FT (88 M²)

COMPLETION
2017

"The cold Canadian climate calls for the design of houses that resemble cocoons," notes designer Jean-Philippe Parent. But the couple that commissioned High House did not desire an old-style chalet; they had lived in the Alps and had been impressed by the minimalism of Swiss architecture. Nor did they want a large second home, but rather a cottage, which would be like a hotel room where they could drop luggage before rushing out to enjoy a weekend away from the city.

The design response by Delordinaire, a Paris- and Montréal-based firm founded by architects from France, Canada, and Australia, was to eliminate storage altogether—there is no basement, no garage. This psychological and functional lightness allowed the creation of a small, more refined volume. The starkly simple cottage stands on skinny, stork-like stilts, not hunkered down against the elements, but seemingly embracing them. The clients gained extra outdoor living space beneath the house—an effect reminiscent of Le Corbusier's white-boxes-on-*pilotis* houses of the 1920s—but here the goal is living in harmony with nature.

The living space is as sparse as a cabin in the woods, in keeping with High House's main function: a place to hang one's hat while not snowshoeing or skiing. Durable and low-maintenance, unfinished marine plywood is used throughout for the floors, wall finish, and built-in furniture.

Snow-white painted concrete panels and corrugated metal roofing clad the floating cube, with its sharp outline defined by a pointy, snow-shedding gable. There is wonderful irony in how the igloo-pure house almost disappears in whiteout conditions, yet inhabitants feel safely raised above the harsh landscape. "Elevated stilt constructions are typically used in warm climates and flood zones," the architects note. "There is more insulation under the house," Parent continues, "but the elevation avoids snow drifts accumulating near the house and keeps the entire house out of moisture in the summer."

By lifting the house above the earth, the architects have opened up magnificent views. To the south lies the St. Lawrence Valley, just where the river broadens below Québec City (home of the world's largest winter carnival). To the west, visible through the floor-to-ceiling living room window, lie the busy ski slopes on Mont-Sainte-Anne, which draw weekenders from town.

High House   185

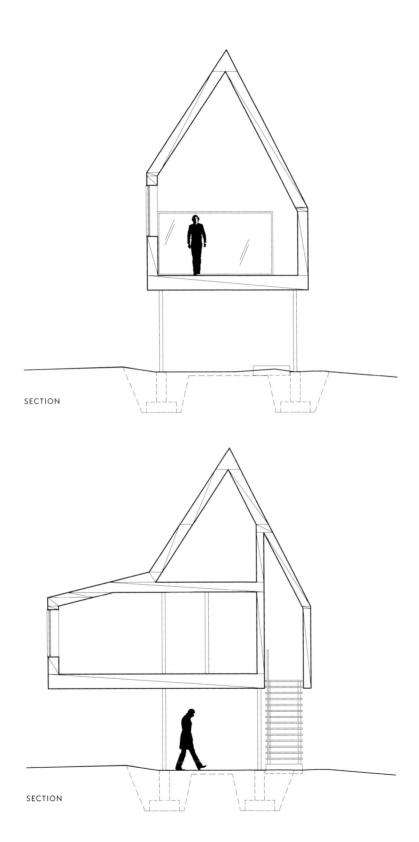

SECTION

SECTION

High House   187

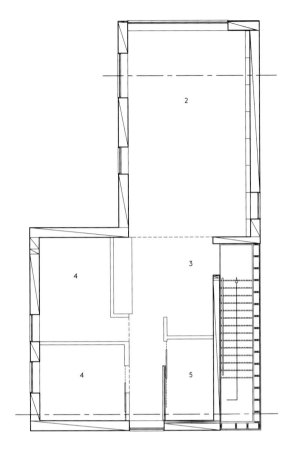

FIRST FLOOR PLAN

10 FT

1   Outdoor area

2   Living space

3   Kitchen

4   Bedroom

5   Bathroom

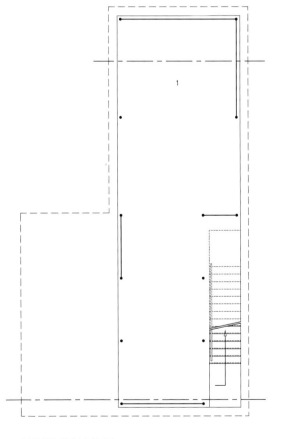

GROUND FLOOR PLAN

La Leonera

LOCATION
Farellones, Chile

ARCHITECT
Del Rio Arquitectos
Asociados (DRAA)

COORDINATES
33.3000 °S
70.2500 °W

AVERAGE WINTER LOW
38°F (-3°C)

ENERGY SYSTEMS
Grid power; gas heat
and hot water

BUILDING MATERIALS
Concrete; timber

SQUARE FOOTAGE
1,076 SQ FT (100 M²)

COMPLETION
2014

A-frame cabins are especially popular in the ski towns of Chile, or as architect Nicolas del Rio notes, they are "one of the most emblematic shelters of the mountains." They are sensible, easily constructed, and energy efficient. The form burst on the second home scene in the 1950s, and was so ubiquitous through the 1970s that the fad became something of a cliché.

Beginning in the 1930s, skiing pioneers built a number of chalets in a variety of mountain styles in Farellones, the oldest and least spoiled of the Chilean ski villages. The first was built by del Rio's grandfather, and now he and design partner Felipe Camus have revived the A-frame in an elegant, bespoke manner.

When La Leonera was unveiled, a critic bemoaned that "A-frames are a classic waste of space," further questioning why the architects would bother "bringing back 1950s bad design." But this one-thousand-square-foot weekend retreat built for designers from the city is more than a nod to nostalgia, as it reinforces the simplicity and straightforwardness of the type. While it is a classic Chilean A-frame, del Rio made the roof more pointed, "in search of a starker image and a loftier feeling inside."

In addition, this new version of the popular form is much more sustainable than its forebears. A polyurethane insulation sandwich covers the pine trusses underneath the zinc roof, creating a robust, continuous thermal barrier. Solar radiation, transmitted through the expansive glass facade, is captured as heat in the thermally massive concrete lower level, which helps dampen temperature swings between day and night.

That base element on which the A-frame sits is a concrete sleigh, "a platform detached from the ground to deliver a lightness." What might at first read as a hackneyed reinterpretation of the A-frame trope is really a sophisticated exploration of two geometric elements. Perching the open, wooden triangle atop its seemingly solid rectangular pedestal and cantilevering it out precipitously over its plinth creates a welcome tension. (At the rear, this overhang covers wood storage for the home's stove).

The typology of the form and its practicality aside, the wisdom of choosing an A-frame design is evident when facing the full-height window that looks out on nothing but the snow-covered Andes.

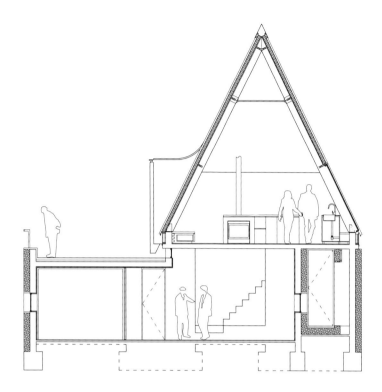

SECTION

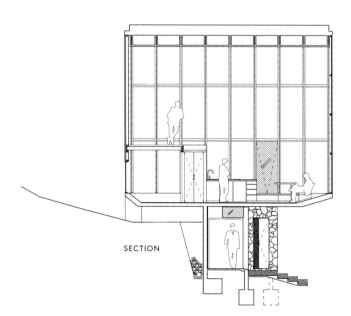

SECTION

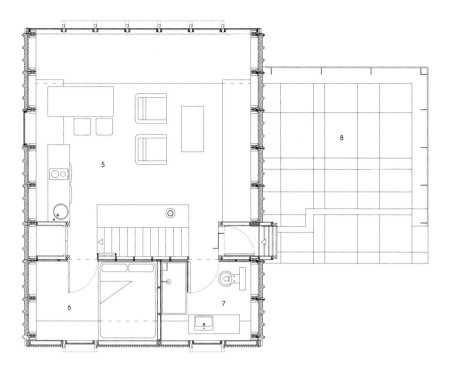

LEVEL TWO PLAN

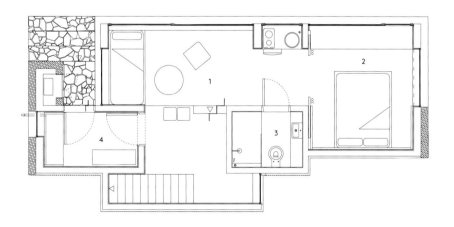

LEVEL ONE PLAN

1   Study
2   Bedroom
3   Toilet
4   Airlock
5   Living area
6   Bedroom
7   Toilet
8   Terrace

10 FT

Rabbit Snare Gorge

LOCATION
Inverness, Nova Scotia

ARCHITECT
Omar Gandhi Architect
in collaboration with
Design Base 8

COORDINATES
46.2308°N
61.3044°W

AVERAGE WINTER LOW
17°F (-8°C)

ENERGY SYSTEMS
Grid power; radiant
in-floor heating

BUILDING MATERIALS
Engineered lumber (framing);
eastern white cedar boards
(cladding); birch plywood
(interior)

SQUARE FOOTAGE
1,200 SQ FT (111 M²)

COMPLETION
2015

Rabbit Snare Gorge was where nearby resident Lawrence MacIsaac's great-grandfather taught his sons how to trap dinner. Here, too, on the rugged coast of Cape Breton Island, MacIsaac's great-grandmother washed her family's clothing on a laundry stone beneath a waterfall. The rocky landscape of "New Scotland" may have seemed familiar to Scots settlers, but it was not fertile soil for farming, and thus this wooded area has not changed much since early settlement. Echoing the steep sides of the gorge, this vacation house rises above forest to gain views of the Gulf of St. Lawrence.

Though stretching skyward to get above the trees, the cabin echoes the local vernacular with its shed form topped by a traditional gable, along with its vertical sheathing of locally sourced white cedar. The variety of window sizes, especially the narrow openings, fulfill the dream of the true environmentalist or the savvy farmer, in that their heliotropic placement was designed to gather as much sunlight as possible. A tower means a smaller footprint, but also allows for a soaring, double-height kitchen.

The tower, nevertheless, is exposed to the ocean, susceptible to downpours, Nor'easters, and corrosive spray from crashing waves, not to mention the winds, which can reach 120 miles per hour. A windbreak of weathering steel hangs on the house's perimeter, and extra sheathing in a reverse board-and-batten pattern provides a system of shear walls, diaphragms, and stacked compression rings for additional protection.

Collaborating architects Design Base 8 and Omar Gandhi provide a modern riff on the relatively plain Cape Breton farmhouse—simple, compact, modest. Yet there is another magical element of Rabbit Snare Gorge: beyond the name, with its evocations of Farmer McGregor and *Watership Down*, the tall skinny house brings to mind children's drawings of houses. Together, sophisticated clients from away—who love the region around the gorge—three young designers, and a Nova Scotia architect created a work of art with a quirky, homegrown sustainability.

This fairy-tale house is experienced by a procession from the rocky ground outside, through a basement level and bedrooms, to the soaring space above the kitchen, and onto the living space at the top. From this aerie one looks out over a landscape barely altered by four centuries of hardscrabble survival to the sea that surrounds this rugged island.

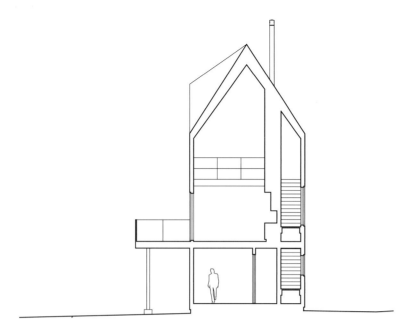

SECTION

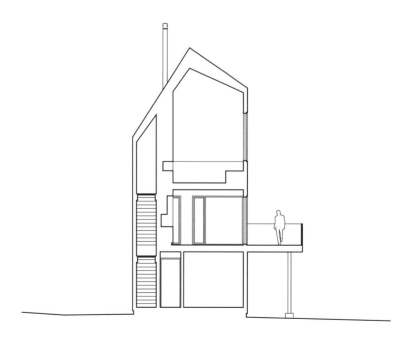

SECTION

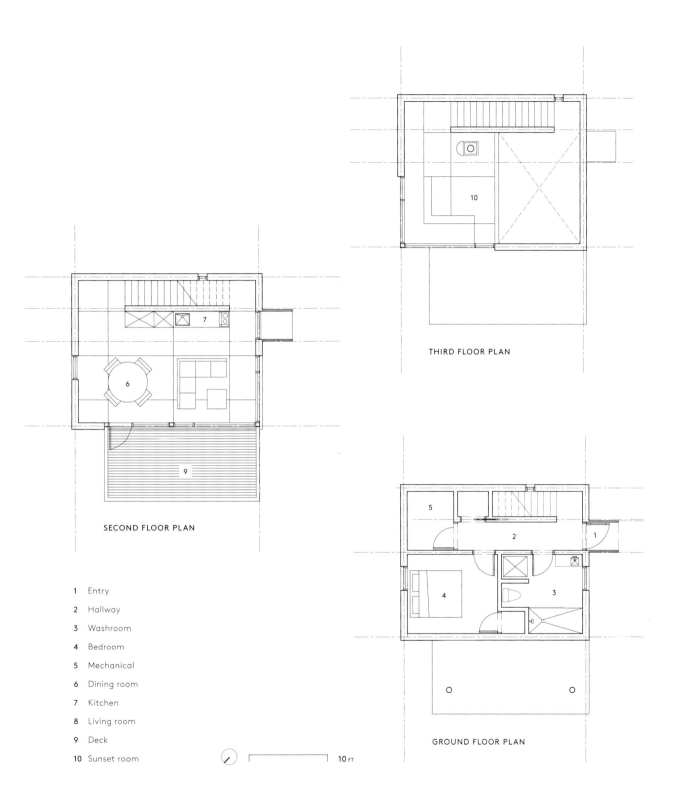

THIRD FLOOR PLAN

SECOND FLOOR PLAN

GROUND FLOOR PLAN

1   Entry
2   Hallway
3   Washroom
4   Bedroom
5   Mechanical
6   Dining room
7   Kitchen
8   Living room
9   Deck
10 Sunset room

10 FT

Culardoch
Shieling

ARCHITECT
Moxon Architects

COORDINATES
57.0607°N
3.6066°W

AVERAGE WINTER LOW
26°F (-3°C)

ENERGY SYSTEMS
Woodburning stove

BUILDING MATERIALS
Scottish larch (exterior
cladding); locally sourced roof
covering; untreated, locally
grown spruce (interior)

SQUARE FOOTAGE
505 SQ FT (47 M²)

COMPLETION
2016

One can hardly imagine a wilder landscape in all of Great Britain than the Cairngorms in the heart of Scotland—a land of moors and romantic vistas. These mountains have magical Gaelic names, like Leabaidh an Dàimh Bhuidhe. Culardoch hut, or *shieling*, is barely visible, hidden down as it is in the deep folds of the hills.

Unlike gentler parts of Scotland, this area has an arctic microclimate. And, while the Cairngorms National Park attracts hikers and campers, its wild topography can be dangerous. While seclusion and a chance to expose guests to raw nature were the clients' goals, the shieling also serves as a publicly accessible emergency shelter for mountaineers that might be caught in an unexpected heavy snowfall.

Erected to serve as a checkpoint for explorers among the granite outcrops, dramatic waterfalls, and mossy riverbeds of the Cairngorms, Culardoch Shieling is a traditional hut that is also an unabashed work of modern design by Moxon Architects. Harsh weather requires that the house hunker down, so that it seems to grow from the earth; the planted roof recalls ancient crofts and farm structures, yet avoids trite Highlands mannerisms. Un-planed and untreated local timber wraps the shieling against the weather.

Simplicity is the watchword inside, where a single Parsons table provides the centerpiece of a long and narrow dining room or hall that suggests the underside of a Viking ship overturned to provide shelter. Accents of handcrafted black steel hinges, table legs, and a suspended ceiling shelf for candles further enhance the aura of a primitive, pre-industrial land. The owners entertain here with decidedly no frills amenities: a single wood stove, a composting toilet, and candlelight (there's no electricity).

Yet, there is a great amount of sophistication amidst the studied austerity. Scattershot windows of different sizes and shapes recall the stained glass chinks in the walls of Le Corbusier's chapel at Ronchamp. From outside at night, the hut reads as a lantern. Chosen by size and orientation to admit light, these deeply inset openings do not breech the required solidity of the walls, but frame specific views of the wild and isolated landscape.

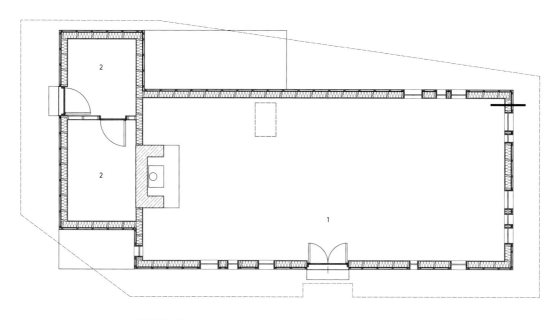

FLOOR PLAN

1 Dining room

2 Storage

10 FT

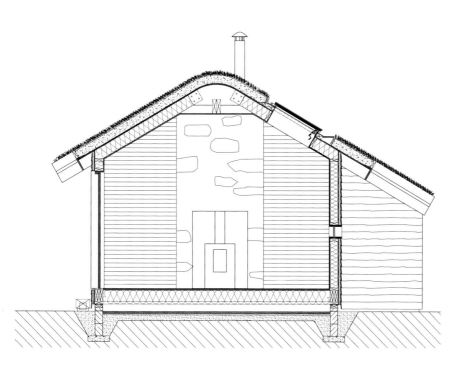

SECTION

Sites

Saint-Ferréol-les-Neiges,
Quebec

Cairngorms,
Scotland

Inverness,
Nova Scotia

Thornton,
New Hampshire

Vancouver Island,
British Columbia

Cornwall,
Connecticut

Eden,
Utah

Grand Marais,
Minnesota

Farellones,
Chile

Okstindan,
Norway

Mylla,
Norway

Kandalaksha,
Russia

Virrat,
Finland

När, Gotland,
Sweden

Embach,
Austria

Manigod,
France

Laterns,
Austria

Fontanella,
Austria

Fukushima,
Japan

Les Grillesses,
Switzerland

Acknowledgments

Any book is the result of a collaboration, and *Snowbound* is no exception. The designers of these twenty projects and their office staffs were exemplary in their helpfulness and enthusiasm. My gratitude to the architects whose work was considered but not ultimately included.

Snowbound was Abby Bussel's idea. She generously trusted me to be her literary doppelgänger. Associate Editor Stephanie Holstein and Production Editor Parker Menzimer considerably lightened my load.

Some years ago, I edited a book about Finnish architects Mikko Heikkinen and Markku Komonen. My essay on these two modern designers and their cultural roots was entitled "One Tight Snowball," a reference to Alvar Aalto's prowess in a snowball fight. Thanks to all my Finn friends, as well as the government of Finland, for encouraging me to embrace winter-clad design.

As always, there would be no book without Carolyn.

William Morgan is the author of numerous books on American architecture, including *The Cape Cod Cottage* and *Monadnock Summer*. He has taught at Princeton University, University of Louisville, and Brown University, and he was a visiting lecturer at Åbo Akademi, Finland's Swedish-language university.

Project Credits

Alpine Cabin
ARCHITECT: Scott & Scott Architects
CONSTRUCTION: Susan and David Scott,
Peter Jensen, Chad Jamison et al.
PHOTOGRAPHY: ©Scott & Scott Architects

Atrium House
ARCHITECT: Tham & Videgård
PROJECT TEAM: Bolle Tham (chief architect),
Tove Belfrage, Martin Videgård
STRUCTURAL ENGINEER: Carl-Uno Pålstedt, Ramböll
PHOTOGRAPHY: ©Åke E:son Lindman

Cabin on a Rock
ARCHITECT: I-Kanda Architects
TEAM: Isamu Kanda, Chris Sledziona, Steven Hien,
Sangsuri Chun
BUILDER PHASE 1: Nest Woodworking
BUILDER PHASE 2: Randy Latulippe Carpentry
STRUCTURAL ENGINEER: Fire Tower Engineered Timber
PREFABRICATED FRAMING: Bensonwood
WINDOWS AND DOORS: Architectural Openings
STAINLESS STEEL KITCHEN, SHOWER, EXTERIOR RAILINGS,
FIREPIT: Seidman Brothers
SITEWORK: Jim Sanborn & Sons
PLUMBING: Squam Lake Plumbing & Heating
ELECTRICAL: Leroy Bixby Electric
PHOTOGRAPHY: ©Matt Delphenich

Cornwall Cabin
ARCHITECT: Resolution: 4 Architecture
PRINCIPALS: Joseph Tanney, Robert Luntz
PROJECT ARCHITECT: Chad Richardson
CONTRACTOR: Richard E. McCue Inc.
MODULAR MANUFACTURING: Simplex Homes
PHOTOGRAPHY: ©Resolution: 4 Architecture

Culardoch Shieling
ARCHITECT: Moxon Architects Ltd
QUANTITY SURVEYOR: McCue & Porter
MAIN CONTRACTOR: AJC Aboyne
CLIENT REPRESENTATIVE: Fowler Fortescue
PHOTOGRAPHY: ©Ben Addy

DublDom
ARCHITECT: Ivan Ovchinnikov and
Pavel Sedov, Russia
TEAM: Ivan Ovchinnikov, Pavel Sedov, Alexandr
Trunkovsky, Fedor Ratnikov, Ilya Barabanov
PHOTOGRAPHY: © Artem Lasovsky

Einfamilienhaus Hochleitner
ARCHITECT: LP architektur
MASTER BUILDER: KAISERER Bau GmbH
CARPENTERING: MEIBERGER HOLZBAU GmbH&COKG
CARPENTER AND JOINER: PAUL HAGENAUER GmbH
PLUMBING INSTALLATION: SCHACHNER Haustechnik
ELECTRIC INSTALLATION: ELEKTROTECHNIK
KONTRINER GmbH
PHOTOGRAPHY: ©Albrecht Schnabel

Four-Cornered Villa
ARCHITECT: Ville Hara and Anu Puustinen,
Avanto Architects Ltd.
STRUCTURAL DESIGN: Konstru Oy and Jorma Eskola
ELECTRICAL DESIGN: Virtain Sähkötyö Oy
and Väinö Sipilä
PHOTOGRAPHY: © Anders Portman

Gaudin House
ARCHITECT: Savoiz Fabrizzi
CIVIL ENGINEERS: Editech SA
HEATING / SANITARY ENGINEERS: Enerconseil SA
MASONRY: Fernando Loureiro
CARPENTRY (ROOF): Philippe Aymon Charpente
CARPENTRY (INTERIOR, WOODEN FURNITURE): Modabois
ROOFING / TINSMITH AND PLUMBER/SANITARY:
Travelletti Biner
FLOOR COVERING: Florent Aymon
PHOTOGRAPHY: ©Thomas Jantscher

Haus Fontanella

ARCHITECT: Bernardo Bader
STATICS: Editech SA
CONSTRUCTION: Dobler Holzbau
CONSTRUCTION MANAGEMENT: Jürgen Haller
WINDOWS: Böhler Fenster
PHOTOGRAPHY: © Albrecht Schnabel

High House

ARCHITECT: DELORDINAIRE
ENGINEER: Latéral, ingénieurs en structure
PHOTOGRAPHY: © Olivier Blouin

Horizon Neighborhood

ARCHITECT: MacKay-Lyons Sweetapple Architects
DESIGN LEAD: Brian MacKay-Lyons
PROJECT ARCHITECTS: Duncan Patterson,
Jennifer Esposito
PROJECT TEAM: Reid Joslin, Matt Jones, Ben Fuglevand,
Farhan Durrani, Paulette Cameron; interior design
by Diana Carl, Sawa Rostkowska
CIVIL CONSULTANT: Talisman Civil Consultants
STRUCTURAL ENGINEER: Dynamic Structures
ELECTRICAL ENGINEER: BNA Engineers
CONSTRUCTION: Mountain Resort Builders Custom
INTERIOR DESIGN: Haley Duffin & Megan Rider for
Powder Mountain
SKETCHES AND DRAWINGS: Brian MacKay-Lyons
DRAWING CREDITS: MacKay-Lyons Sweetapple Architects
PHOTOGRAPHY: © Younes Bounhar, Doublespace
Photography (146–147, 148, 150, 152–153)
© Paul Bundy (145, 154–155)

La Leonera

ARCHITECT: Del Rio Architectos Asociados (DRAA)
ARCHITECTS IN CHARGE: Nicolas del Rio and Felipe
Camus
COLLABORATORS: Matthias J. Götz, Malo Chabrol
CONSTRUCTION: Handitu Ltda.
STRUCTURAL ENGINEER: ARBEC
PHOTOGRAPHY: © Filipe Camus

Mountain Cabin

ARCHITECT: Marte.Marte
CONTRACTOR: Amann Bau
CONCRETE WORKS: Weikelstorfer
STRUCTURAL CONSULTANT: Frick Paul
WINDOWS: Hartmann
CONSTRUCTION PHYSICS: Bernhard Weithas
FAT ROOF: Tectum
FURNISHINGS / INTERIOR FITTINGS: Matt Gerold
HEATING / SANITATION: Gangl Manfred
ELECTRICAL SERVICES: Matt Thomas
STAIRS: Türtscher Kaspar
PHOTOGRAPHY: © Marc Lins

Mountain House

ARCHITECT: Studio Razavi Architecture
PRINCIPAL: Alireza Razavi
PROJECT MANAGER: Andoni Briones
MEP: Emenda
PHOTOGRAPHY: © Olivier Martin-Gambier (13, 16, 18–19)
© Simone Bossi (15)

Mylla Hytte

ARCHITECT: Mork-Ulnes Architects
PROJECT DESIGN TEAM: Auste Cijunelyte, Tom Erdman,
Lexie Mork-Ulnes, Casper Mork-Ulnes, Anatoly Starr
GENERAL CONTRACTOR: Michal Manzak and Konrad
Jasinski, Kreativt Hus
PHOTOGRAPHY: © Bruce Damonte

One Year Project

ARCHITECT: ADX
PROJECT MANAGER: Kotaro Anzai
ENGINEER: Kenji Nawa / Nawakenji-m
CONSTRUCTION: ADX
PHOTOGRAPHY: © ADX

Rabbit Snare Gorge

ARCHITECT: Omar Gandhi Architect in collaboration with Design Base 8
FIRM CREDITS: Omar Gandhi, Principal,
Peter Braithwaite, Intern Architect,
Peter Kolodziej, Intern Architect,
Maxwell Schnutgen, Intern Architect,
Elizabeth Powell, Intern Architect,
Jeff Shaw, Intern Architect,
In collaboration with
Jon Siani, Intern Architect, Design Base 8
Jon Wilson, Intern Architect,
Garrett Helm, Intern Architect,
PHOTOGRAPHY: ©Younes Bounhar,
Doublespace Photography

Rabothytta

ARCHITECT: Jarmund / Vigsnæs Arkitekter
PRIMARY ARCHITECTS: Einar Jarmund, Håkon Vigsnæs,
Alessandra Kosberg, Ane Sønderaal Tolfsen
CONSULTANTS: Walter Jacobsen MNT, RAMBØLL AS, MBA
Entreprenør AS
PHOTOGRAPHY: ©Svein Arne Brygfjeld (85, 86),
©Jan Inge Larsen (81, 82–83, 88, 89, 90–91)
©Tommy Eliassen (92–93) ©Einar Aslaksen (87)

Tre Søstre

ARCHITECT: Salmela Architect
PRINCIPAL AND DESIGNER: David Salmela, FAIA
DESIGN TEAM: Darin Duch
ENGINEER: Meyer Borgman Johnson
LANDSCAPE: Travis Van Liere Studio
CONTRACTOR: Taiga Design+Build
PHOTOGRAPHY: ©Corey Gaffer

Published by
Princeton Architectural Press
202 Warren Street
Hudson, New York 12534
www.papress.com

© 2021 Princeton Architectural Press
All rights reserved.
Printed and bound in China
24 23 22 21 4 3 2 1 First edition

Editor: Parker Menzimer
Cover design: Paul Wagner
Designer: Paula Baver

Library of Congress Cataloging-in-Publication Data

Names: Morgan, William, 1944- author.
Title: Snowbound : dwelling in winter / William Morgan.
Description: First edition. | New York : Princeton
     Architectural Press, 2020. | Summary: "Tour twenty
     beautiful, elemental, and sustainable winter residences
     and shelters across the globe from the US to Japan"—
     Provided by publisher.
Identifiers: LCCN 2020004436 | ISBN 9781616898670
Subjects: LCSH: Architect-designed houses. | Architecture,
     Domestic—Cold regions.
Classification: LCC NA7117.C64 M67 2020 | DDC 728—dc23
LC record available at https://lccn.loc.gov/2020004436